CW00616046

Published by Oast Publishing, The Old Dairy, Street Farm, Ulcombe,
Nr Maidstone, Kent ME17 1DP. Tel: 01622 842988

ISBN: 978-0-9956895-1-0

Bible Stories:
telling it slant

by Molly Poulter

illustrated by Pauline Appleton

Contents

Preface

One of the tasks every generation of believers takes on is how to bring the familiar stories of scripture to life. Although there are generations now emerging for whom they are unknown and fresh, those who have heard them throughout childhood and had them explained in innumerable sermons, aren't coming to them to find out what happened. They know all too well what happened interminably.

How can these wonderful stories regain their fresh, life changing dynamism? How can they be heard not for information but for transformation? How can they enter the heart and turn it ninety degrees? How can we re-capture the fascination, shock and sheer enjoyment of the original hearers?

The answer often lies in scraping off the familiar layers of the known text and digging in to the lived experience as it would have been when Jesus was present. What we need is what our American cousins would call the 'baptised imagination', a re-telling which holds to the text but then imagines more. And this is what Molly Poulter does in these delightful pieces.

Molly clearly loves these stories. And she loves them too much to leave them languishing unexplored and un-enjoyed. What she has done with them is what any of us can do if we let ourselves off the leash. May she be our inspiration as she unpacks the surface of the narratives and lets them sparkle afresh in our privileged hands.

+ John Pritchard

1. The Christmas Present

The little kitten lay huddled in the straw. He was very frightened and very hungry. He hadn't eaten for three days – not since his mother had come limping back to the barn without anything to eat. She'd stretched out beside him and he'd snuggled up to her to get warm and had fallen asleep. When he woke, she was still there – but lying very still and cold.

He heard the loud voices of the farmer and his son as they entered the barn and had scuttled away to hide because his mother had warned him that the man didn't like cats. He felt very sad that he was too small to hide his mother, for he knew the farmer had prying eyes and would soon see her lying there.

"Another dead cat," the voice exclaimed. " We've got far too many of them around the place. Good riddance, say I – but don't let your mum know I said so." He saw the farmer bend down and pick up his mother and carry her away – he knew not where.

He was very brave and didn't cry out – but lay there still – just as his mother had taught him.

Since then, three days had passed, and he was getting colder and more and more hungry and lonely. There were other animals in the barn – but they lived at the other end, and were so big and noisy that he was frightened of them. And he knew they wouldn't give him anything to eat – they didn't seem to eat the same things his mother had given him.

He lay there feeling very sorry for himself. Apart from the steady munching of the cows, it was all very quiet. Through the open door of the barn he could see the moon shining very brightly. His mother had told him about the moon. It was the light that shone at night, she had said It was not so bright as the sun which gave light in the day, and not nearly so warm.

But somehow, though he'd seen the moon before, everything looked different – the ground was sparkling and white. Had his mother been there, he would have ventured out to explore as he was a very inquisitive kitten, but without her there to give him confidence, and call him back at the right moment, he didn't dare leave the warm straw.

Suddenly the quiet was broken by the sound of voices and he saw a small group of people coming through the open doorway. He quickly hid under the straw

'Well, here it is," said the farmer. "That's the best I can do for you. It isn't very comfortable, but at least it's dry and out of the cold. There's a well at the end of the barn if you want water, and I'll shut the door to keep out the wind and the snow."

The farmer left – but the kitten saw that his wife, a kind lady, had stayed behind to help the little group – a man and a woman and a small pony. The man took the pony to the other end of the barn and tied it up with the cows, while the farmer's wife fussed round the lady, and tried to make her comfortable in the straw.

Being just a little kitten, and weak from lack of food, he soon dozed off again and missed all the bustle and excitement of the next two hours. But he was woken by the sound of a baby's cry. Peering out from the straw he saw that one of the boxes that held the cow's food had been moved. The cry was coming from that direction and he could see that the farmer, his wife, and the man, were all looking down into it with an expression of wonder and happiness.

Being an inquisitive kitten, he desperately wanted to see what they were looking at, but was too weak from hunger to move.

He heard the noise of the big barn doors opening, and for a moment the moon shone brightly on the scene. Then it was obscured as five men walked into the barn. Unlike the farmer they had gentle voices and he heard them asking where the babe was. The farmer's wife waved them over and pointed to the stall. The five men walked hesitantly across the barn and peered into the stall – and immediately knelt down and bent their heads.

For a moment, a great silence fell on the barn and the kitten shivered – not with fear but with a sort of excitement. Then suddenly, the silence was broken by the bleating of a small lamb and the kitten noticed that one of the men had a tiny lamb in his arms and was feeding it from a sponge. What was even more interesting to the kitten was the fact that milk was spilling out from the sponge onto the straw.

The little kitten's hunger was now so great, and the sight of the milk so tempting, that he overcame his fear and slipped out from under the straw, and crept over to where the baby lay, and tried to catch the drips from the sponge.

But though he'd tried to be as quiet and stealthy as his mother had taught him, one of the men caught sight of him and picked him up.

"A kitten!" he exclaimed. "Where's its mother?"

The farmer's wife looked round quickly. "Oh dear," she said, "My husband found a dead female cat here the other day – but he didn't say there were any kittens. It must be starving. That was all of three day's ago."

The man with the lamb silently handed over the sponge that the lamb had been sucking and within seconds, the kitten was happily sucking the drops of milk that dripped from the sponge.

Satisfied at last, comforted by the warmth of the man's body, the kitten was ready to snuggle down to sleep – but not before he had seen what was in the stall. He crept onto the shoulder of the man and looked down. There, lying in the stall, was a tiny baby, and the light shining around him was like the light that came from the moon – only it was warm like the light of the sun. And the little kitten purred with wonder.

The man stroked the kitten gently and, turning to the farmer's wife. said, "You won't be wanting to keep this little kitten if its mother's dead. Can I take it home with me and give it to my daughter as a present?"

The farmer's wife smiled and nodded.

"We must be going, ma'm," said the men to the lady lying in the straw. "But thank'ee for letting us see your Baby. He's very special. Us must give thanks to God for His birth," and they gently placed the lamb in the arms of the lady.

They turned and walked quietly out of the barn – and one of the men was carrying in his arms the first Christmas present for his daughter – a little kitten.

Matthew 2.vv10-11

2. The Wedding

When Lila opened her eyes and saw the sun dancing on the windowsill, she knew immediately that the day was special. There was a tension in the air, and the room somehow looked different as it always did when something exciting was about to happen.

She leapt out of bed, pulled back the curtains and looked out of the window. Nothing was stirring – just a few chickens pecking their way along the roadside and the neighbour's cat lying in its usual sleepy pose on top of the garden wall.

She gazed slowly round the room trying to remember what it was that had caused this feeling of excitement. Then her glance fell on the white dress draped across the chair under the window – and remembered. Today was her cousin Rachel's wedding day – and she was to be a bridesmaid.

It was going to be a great occasion. All the village folk would be there and there would be feasting and music and dancing. Lila had been looking forward to this day for a long time and now at last it had arrived.

She wanted to put on the dress straight away but remembered, just in time, that the festivities wouldn't begin till much later in the day. She knew just what her mother would say if she wore it now, and could hear in anticipation her mother's voice warning her not to get it dirty.

So she washed and dressed thoughtfully and decided to put on her oldest dress which had a tear across the sleeve.

When she came down to breakfast her brother had left already. He was to be the bridegroom's best man and would be spending the day with him and all his attendants until the time came for them to go over to the bride's house.

Lila felt a tinge of envy. She would have to wait till much later before she could go to Rachel's house. She was only the littlest bridesmaid, and her mother had said that Rachel would want to spend time with her grown-up bridesmaids and wouldn't want Lila trailing around behind her all morning. Lila would have to find something to do until it was time to get ready.

Finishing her breakfast, Lila washed her plate and decided to go and find her friend Sarah.

Calling good-bye to her mother, Lila skipped along the village street until she came to Sarah's house – whitewashed just like her own, but with some large ceramic pots outside.

Sarah ran out to greet her, and the two girls made their way to the workplace of their special friend who lived at the other end of the village – hoping he would be back from his travels as he'd promised.

On their way they stopped to talk to Matilda who was sitting outside her front door, working on a large quilt; they peered in at the book shop and saw Amos sitting there looking grumpy as he usually did; they waved at Thomas the greengrocer who laughed and threw them two oranges which they chased after down the street; and they passed Deborah's house and saw her busy at work, baking for the wedding feast that night.

Nearing their special friend's workshop, they realised he wasn't there, and felt very disappointed. Before he'd gone away, they'd spent hours watching him at work and listening to him talk. He never grumbled, never pretended to be cross or too busy, and always seemed to have plenty of time for them. It wasn't that he stopped working while they were with him. He kept on gently fashioning whatever it was he was working on, the sawdust gradually piling up on the floor under his workbench, while he told them the most marvellous stories about people and animals and birds, and the fields all around them. Somehow, even though he didn't suggest it, the stories always made them want to go home and be kind and helpful to their families.

But last year he had gone away and left them. They'd begged him to stay but he'd told them, very gently, that he had to go and do some business for his Father. It had been the very day when Lila knew she was to be a bridesmaid at her cousin's wedding, and she and Sara had rushed to tell him the news. They cried when he said he was going away, but he said he would be back for the wedding, and would see them then. He explained all the things that happened at a wedding and what they meant, and he told Lila what a very important job she had to do as her cousin's bridesmaid, and how she must do her very best to make it a happy day for Rachel. Then shaking off the sawdust, he had gently laid his hands on their heads, and sent them on their way.

But today he wasn't there – and Lila and Sarah, disappointed, retraced their steps to their homes.

It seemed an eternity before the time came for Lila to wash and put on the lovely white bridesmaid's dress. Then, with her mother beside her, she walked along the street to Rachel's house, clutching in her hand the little posy of flowers and the tiny lamp which would later show the bridegroom the way to Rachel's house. It puzzled her a little to think that the bridegroom needed a lamp as she'd seen him at Rachel's house many times in the past. But her mother said that it was an ancient custom – and who was she to argue with her mother.

They arrived at Rachel's house to find it was full of people, all chattering away nineteen to the dozen. Some of the younger ones were dressed just like herself, but Lila felt important because she was the only little one there – and Rachel had told her that she was her very special bridesmaid.

Lila watched as the older bridesmaids helped Rachel get ready. They gently rubbed perfumed oil into her hair and on her arms, neck and shoulder. Then they helped her put on her dress – the most beautiful Lila had ever seen. And they laced up her sandals and placed flowers in her hair. And Rachel gave Lila the very special task of fastening the head-dress with all the coins on it which her father had given her when she was betrothed.

Every now and then, Lila gave a little skip of excitement. There was such joy and laughter in the room that Lila couldn't remember ever before feeling so happy and so important.

The light began to fade rapidly and suddenly one of the maidservants entered the room and said, 'The bridegroom's coming'. Everyone rushed outside, and the bridesmaids lined up on either side of the door, and the maidservant came along with a lighted taper and lit the oil in their lamps.

Lila could hear the sound of the bridegroom's party approaching. There was music and laughter and clapping – and then she could see them – lanterns swaying and the bridegroom leading the procession, with her own brother walking beside him, and all the attendants following behind.

It seemed to Lila that there wouldn't be room in the house for all of them – but somehow they all squeezed in, and then came the exchange of presents which were all placed on a table specially set aside for them.

Then, her brother calling for order, the whole party left the house and processed down the street to the bridegroom's house – lanterns swaying, the bridesmaids' little oil lamps flickering gently in the darkness, music playing and everyone talking and laughing .

The bridegroom's house was only in the next street but it was a big house because the bridegroom's father was an important man in the village.

Lila knew that she had to be very quiet for the next part of the ceremony, because it was then that Rachel and the bridegroom would make their vows as husband and wife. The rabbi was waiting for them, robed in his best and most colourful robes. Rachel and the bridegroom stood before him, and Rachel's parents and family, and the groom's parents and family, and all the groom's attendants, and Rachel's bridesmaids, stood round as the rabbi solemnly read out the marriage contract.

Then the groom, looking at Rachel, said in a clear voice, 'She is my wife and I am her husband from this day and forever' and everyone said, 'May the God of heaven keep you safe and give you prosperity.'

Then there was a lot of kissing and hugging, and more people started coming in through the door, and within a short time it seemed as though the whole village had come into the house – Deborah the cook, old Matilda, Thomas the greengrocer, and even grumpy old Amos. She saw with delight her special friend across the room. He had come, just as he'd promised. He was with his mother and some men she didn't know, but when he saw Lila he gave her a little wave and a smile, and she knew he would come and talk to her when he could – and Lila gave a little skip of joy

Everyone was given a glass of wine, and even the children were allowed to drink a glassful that had been watered down. Lila didn't like it very much, but as she was now very thirsty, she gulped it down quickly. It had been a long day, and she was beginning to feel both tired and hungry, and her spirits lifted when she saw huge platefuls of food being brought in by the servants.

Everyone rushed towards the food, and crowded round the tables. Because she was so small Lila was able to squeeze through the throng and get right up to one of the tables. She helped herself from the plates nearest to her, and started to eat.

When she had eaten to the full, she squeezed her way from the table and looked round for somewhere to sit – but all the chairs were occupied. There were speeches and dancing, and lots of drinking, and the noise got louder and louder, and Lila began to feel more and more sleepy. She felt overwhelmed by the noisy crowd around her, and some of the men were getting a bit rough, and Lila felt afraid of them. She couldn't see her mother anywhere, while Rachel and her husband were at the other end of the room, and there was no way she could squeeze her way through to them.

Then she spied some very large jars, almost as tall as herself, in the corner of the room, and pushing her way through the crowd, found a space behind them and stretched herself out, and within moments had drifted off into sleep.

She was woken by some agitated whispering. It was the servants. She could hear the sound of vessels scraping the inside of the large jars in front of her. ''It's no good. It's all been drunk. There's nothing left. I'm afraid our master has made a bad mistake. He's just going to have to tell his guests it's all gone'

Then Lila heard another say, 'He'll lose face with his friends and neighbours – and he's not going to be at all pleased with us,'

Lila, peeping through the gaps between the jars, noticed her special friend's mother standing nearby, and remembered that they were cousins of the bridegroom's family. She heard her say gently to one of the servants, 'You seem anxious. Is there a problem?'

One of the servants said, 'It's a nightmare. All the wine's been drunk – and the evening has only just begun. I don't know what our master is going to say to us when he finds out.'

She said to them, 'Wait awhile' and Lila watched her walk across the room to where

her special friend was standing. She saw them whispering together, and her special friend shook his head, and seemed to be arguing with his mother.

Then she came back to the servants, who were still standing by the large stone jars, and said to them, 'Do whatever he tells you.'

Then her special friend came over, and said to the servants, 'Fill all six jars to the brim with water.'

Lila was getting cramped and wanted to stretch and go and find her mother, but she had the strange feeling that she must stay and not let anyone know she was there.

The servants started filling the jars with water, which they carried across in large bowls that were so much wider than the mouths of the jars that lots of the water splashed over the edge and onto Lila as she sat crouched on the ground. Her beautiful dress was getting wetter and wetter, but some force seemed to keep her pinned to the ground.

When all the jars were full, her special friend came over and said to the servants, 'Now, draw some off and take it to the master of the feast.'

Lila watched as one of the servants drew off a glass of wine and took it across to the master. He took a sip, and then Lila watched as he went across to the bridegroom and, slapping him warmly on the shoulder, said loudly. 'Well done my friend. Everyone else serves the best wine first, and the poorer only when the guests have drunk freely, but you have kept the best wine till now." And everyone cheered and the music became more lively than before.

And as Lila watched all this jollity, she heard her name being spoken, and there, looking over the tops of the jars, was her special friend. 'Come, little one. It's been a wonderful day for you. But I think the time has come for you to find your mother and go home to bed.' And lifting her gently in his arms, he carried her across the room to her mother.

John 2: vv1-10

3. Joseph

Joseph couldn't recall a time when he hadn't felt hungry. He'd been wandering the streets for as long as he could remember, and had anyone ever bothered to ask how old he was, he wouldn't have been able to tell them.

He only knew his name because it was one he had chosen himself, having once heard a wandering story-teller recounting the story of a man long ago, called Joseph, who had been thrown into a pit by his jealous brothers, and left to die. Joseph had stopped to hear the rest of the story, and was encouraged to learn that the man had survived his ordeal, and had become Pharaoh's chief minister in Egypt. The boy decided, then and there, to adopt the name Joseph for himself, thinking it might be lucky, but he wasn't too sure that, if he had been Joseph, he would have wanted to help his brothers when they came seeking his help in Egypt during the famine in their own country.

Joseph certainly didn't feel very forgiving of his father. He'd beaten him nearly every day before abandoning him altogether. Of his mother, he had only a faint memory and never thought about her – except on those rare occasions when a certain scent on a woman passer-by evoked a fleeting memory of someone warm and gentle.

Joseph had no fixed resting place, though there were four or five places in the city where he felt more confident of finding scraps of food. People very seldom gave him money, and he never hoped for any. The beggars in the city were too numerous, and he was too small to compete with the older beggars. But he usually managed to forage and collect a few scraps of food when among a throng of beggars, and that's why he often made his way to the five great arches where a crowd of beggars, many crippled and disfigured, waited for the pool to bubble into life.

Tradition had it that the bubbling waters were called into life by a visiting angel, and whoever managed to get first into the pool after the visitation would be cured.

Joseph didn't believe in the angel and thought he knew better. For he'd observed that the pool seemed to surge after a heavy downpour of rain. He wasn't the only one with that opinion, for he noticed that the crowd of beggars and cripples always increased following a cloudburst.

The arches were always crowded – not only with the cripples, but also with a number of spectators, because this was one of the well-known tourist spots in the city. That's why Joseph made his way there if he was particularly hungry because he was hopeful some of the tourists would give him food.

Over the years, Joseph had got to know the cripples at the pool, and soon realised that not all were as ill as they made out. He often sat with Ezra – not because he particularly liked him but because he was so disfigured that the tourists were more generous to him than to some of the others. But none of them were prepared to touch Ezra or lift him into the pool, so Ezra lingered on year after year under the arches by the pool.

This wait hadn't made him a nice companion. He'd become malicious and spiteful, and often complained that his disfigurement prevented him from being a successful pickpocket. But his disabilities didn't prevent him from putting out his stick and tripping over the unwary tourist who got too close – and then leaning over and emptying his pocket while the tourist struggled to get up. He was so clever at this that few tourists ever suspected that it was 'poor Ezra' who had robbed them.

One day, after the waters had bubbled into life and Ezra had once more been left behind in the rush to get into the pool, Joseph noticed a man standing quietly under the one of the great arches, watching what was going on. He was dressed very simply, and there was something about the man that made Joseph forget about scrabbling for food. He watched him closely. The man's gaze was both compassionate and searching, and Joseph, in some indefinable way, felt drawn to him.

The crowd round the pool started to drift away and soon only Joseph and Ezra and a few beggars were left. The man walked over and standing beside Ezra asked him, "Do you want to get well?'

Ezra looked up, and seeing the expression on the man's face, dropped his usual surly expression and said, in a complaining but subservient voice, "Sir, I have no one to put me in the pool when the water's disturbed; while I am getting there, someone else steps into the pool before me."

The man looked at Ezra thoughtfully for a few moments, then said, "Stand up Ezra. Take up your bed and walk."

The man had such authority in his voice that Ezra immediately did as he was bidden and stood up. He took a few tentative steps forward, then realising that he could indeed walk, started walking round the pool more confidently, with a look of amazement on his face.

The man was still looking at him intently, and Ezra remembered the second part of the command, and bent down and picked up his bed roll.

Joseph stood open mouthed with astonishment. He looked for the man – and saw him slipping away behind the arches. He felt a sense of loss and wanted to run after him, but somehow knew that he must stay by Ezra and support him.

As if by magic, a crowd of people began to gather and ask what had happened. Ezra had to repeat the story over and over again, and soon Joseph noticed among the crowd some Pharisees who started questioning Ezra closely. Then one of them said, 'Today's the Sabbath. Don't you know it's against the law to carry your bed?'

Joseph felt indignant and wanted to shout at them for their question but kept quiet because he knew they could cause trouble for him if he said anything. Ezra justified himself to the Pharisees by telling them that he had only done what the man who cured him had told him to do.

The Pharisees asked all sorts of questions, and wanted to know the name of the man who had cured him, but Ezra didn't know, nor could any of the bystanders help.

'Well,' said the Pharisees at last, "when you see him again, ask his name and come and tell us," and Ezra nodded his head

For the next few days Joseph stuck closely by Ezra. People were eager to hear about Ezra's miraculous cure, and Ezra, aware of the advantages to be gained from being reluctant to tell his story, asked for food and donations before he would tell them anything. Joseph, sticking close to Ezra, was also fed.

One morning, Joseph and Ezra found themselves in the temple. Ezra was telling his story to a small crowd when Joseph felt a strange sensation of being watched. He looked up and there was the man observing Ezra closely. He went up to Ezra, and after greeting him said, with a stern look on his face, 'Now that you are well, you must give up your sinful ways or something worse will happen to you.'

Ezra looked startled, and then furtive, and said nothing. Joseph felt angry with Ezra, and wished he would say thank you to the man for his cure. But all Ezra did was to mumble something and shuffle away.

The man turned away looking sad. Joseph was about to go up to him, and speak to him, but two of the man's friends came along and gestured towards a group of people on the other side of the temple. The man, putting his arms across their shoulders, walked away and joined the group.

Joseph had a feeling of loss, but his attention was soon caught by the Pharisees who had asked Ezra about the man who'd healed him. Ezra saw them at the same moment, and walked straight across to them. 'I know who it was who cured me ... ' leaving the rest of the sentence hanging in the air as he held out his hands for some money. The Pharisees looked angry – then one of them put his hands in his pocket, and threw a coin at Ezra.

'That's the man who cured me,' said Ezra, pointing

across the temple to the man who was now surrounded by a crowd of people listening attentively to what he was saying. 'That's him.'

The Pharisees looked triumphant. Joseph felt sure they meant harm to the man, and was angry with Ezra for betraying the man's identity. He decided he would have nothing more to do with him.

He made his way across the temple, and tried to push through the throng crowding round the man. But he was too small, and he watched with disappointment as the man and his friends moved away and disappeared from sight.

Joseph felt empty. His stomach was rumbling with hunger, and he was assailed by a feeling of loneliness such as he'd never felt before. He walked sadly off to find shelter for the night and began to wonder whether his life would ever get better.

It was not till a few days later that Joseph caught up again with the man and his friends. He saw the man's friends first. They were trying to disperse a group of small children who were pestering them for information. Then the man appeared, and told them off for trying to send the children away. He said something about children and heaven, and that the men should become like little children themselves. Joseph wasn't at all sure that would be a good idea, but when all the children sat down on the ground in expectation of a story, Joseph sat down on the ground with them.

Joseph had often before listened to wayside storytellers, but this man's stories were the best he'd ever heard – and somehow they made him think about his life and what he was going to do with it. For the first time he could remember, Joseph had a feeling of hope.

When the story telling finished and the children began to disperse, Joseph felt the man's eyes upon him. 'Joseph,' he called.

Joseph had never told anyone before the name by which he called himself. His eyes filled with tears and all the sorrows of his life came pouring out as he walked into the outspread arms of the man, and knew that from that time on, whatever life had in store for him, he had a friend who would love and care for him always.

John 5: vv. 1-15
Mark 10:vv. 13-16

4. The Leper

At the beginning, he would walk every Sabbath towards the village, and would stand on the little hillock, well outside the village where he'd grown up. He would wait for the brief moment when he could see them walking, hand in hand, towards the synagogue. They would turn towards him, and raise their hands in greeting, before moving through the door, and he knew it would be another whole week before he would see them again.

Then, as the years went by, it seemed more and more hopeless, and he came less frequently to the little hillock. He watched as his little daughter grew into a young woman, and knew he would not recognise her if they'd been able to meet. He hoped and prayed that his lovely wife would find happiness – and, painful though the thought was, he hoped that she might even be allowed to divorce him and make a new life for herself. He had accepted long ago that they would never be able to come together again. He knew there was no cure for the disease – that it never lets up its insidious process of destruction. Already, parts of his fingers were falling off, and the end of his nose was disintegrating.

He found it difficult to forgive God for what he had done to him. But he knew he must – for had he not been told often by the rabbi that he must 'love the Lord your God with all your heart and with all your soul, and with all your might.'

He often felt that life was not worth living. His only companions were fellow sufferers – and many of them were so angry with God they were quite violent. Others had given up any sense of being, and sat huddled in their makeshift shelters, not bothering to try and find food, or make even a semblance of life for themselves.

He thought back to his happy childhood. He had loving parents, and two brothers who had always been willing to play with him and take him off to their place of work. Though the family were Samaritans, his parents kept from him the prejudice of the villagers where they lived.

He thought of his childhood sweetheart, Rachel, who had become his bride. Remembering his wedding was a source of both comfort and despair. It had been such a happy day, with feasting and dancing into the early hours.

Ezra recalled the happy faces of both his and Rachel's parents, who had encouraged the love that was growing between them from a very early age. Rachel's parents had been generous with her dowry, which had enabled them to build a little house for themselves before their marriage.

Their first child arrived just ten months after the wedding. She was a beautiful baby with dark eyes and little curls that framed her face. She had a sunny temperament, and they named her Rina, which means joy.

Ezra worked as a potter in a little workshop just behind their house. He'd learnt his trade from his father from an early age.

Ezra loved his work, and, as well as making simple pots and plates for the local villagers, he would also create some special pieces which he sold to passing travellers. Because he worked from his home, he saw a lot more of Rina than did many fathers. She would toddle into his workshop and pick up a lump of clay, and start modelling. As she grew older, she became more proficient, and produced little pots like her father.

As they worked side by side, he would tell her stories from the Hebrew Scriptures – for he knew God had told Moses that he must recite these words to his children. So he told her about Joseph and his many coloured coat, and his wicked brothers who sold him into slavery. 'But,' said Ezra, 'God was looking after him and he became the Egyptian king's most important minister.' He told her about Ruth who loved her mother-in-law so much that she went to live with her in a foreign land; about David and how he slew Goliath with a single stone, and later was chosen as king.

One of her favourite stories was about the boy, Samuel – how, as he lay in bed, he heard a voice calling him, and thought it was the priest, Eli. But Eli sent him back to bed because he hadn't called him. Samuel heard his name being called a third time, and Eli the priest told him it must be God who was calling him. And Rina would lie in bed and wonder whether she would ever hear God's voice calling her, and would listen very carefully in the darkness.

The story she didn't like was of Daniel being thrown into a lions' den. She would wake in the night sobbing, 'Daddy, don't let them throw you to the lions!' and Ezra would hold her in his arms and tell her that God didn't let the lions eat Daniel, and that he certainly wouldn't let any lions hurt him because He was a loving God – and she would fall asleep again, reassured.

Rina's favourite story was of Noah's Ark, and Ezra started modelling an ark for her in secret. Each day he would ask her to name an animal she thought went into the ark, and that night, after she had gone to bed, he would start moulding the clay into the animal she had chosen. It was a task which gave him great joy.

He loved his wife, Rachel, and she encouraged the time he spent with Rina. Their life was very happy, and their only disappointment was that Rachel failed to conceive again. They had both hoped for a large family – but accepted that this was not God's will.

Then, one day, as he was throwing a pot, he noticed a sore on one of his fingers. His hands had been feeling very cold for a week or two, and he'd lost the sensation of touch. He didn't pay much attention to it – thinking it was because his hands were tired from doing too much potting. But, seeing the sore, he felt a shudder going through his body. He remembered what people had told him about leprosy – how it started with a loss of temperature, and then a loss of sensation, and then the tell-tale sores appeared. And he remembered, too, all the frightening passages in Leviticus about leprosy – which explained how leprosy was to be identified. The passages talked about skin that was white, and hair that was white, and sores that had a spot of raw flesh in the middle.

For the next week, he was very quiet, and kept himself to himself. As he sat in his little workshop, he prayed to God that it was just a sore that would heal quickly. But in his heart of hearts, he knew it was leprosy. At night, he avoided contact with his wife – saying he was very tired, and when Rachel asked him what was wrong, he insisted it was just exhaustion because he had been working so hard. And when Rina came into the workshop, instead of holding her close as he usually did, he kept her at a distance, knowing that leprosy could be passed on by touch.

He watched the sore time and time again in the hope it would go away – but instead, it got bigger and bigger – and one morning he saw with horror that there was a spot of blood in the middle of the sore – and the hairs round it had turned white. And then he discovered a sore on the other hand, and one on his feet – and he knew he was a leper.

He put his head in his hands and wept.

He knew he would have to go to the priest who would examine him. He knew the procedure. He had known people who had become lepers. He knew the priest would examine the sores and if they were white and had a spot of raw flesh in the swelling, he would be pronounced a leper, unclean, and would be banned from all contact with his family and friends and the whole community.

He knew, too, that once the leprosy took hold, it would eat away his body, and he would lose his fingers and his nose, his feet, and the flesh on his face.

He didn't tell Rachel beforehand – but crept away early in the morning. The priest he saw was a kindly man who examined him gently – but after looking very carefully at the sores he said, with a very sad expression, 'Ezra, my son there is no doubt this is leprosy. I must pronounce you unclean. You must go home and say farewell to your family – and join the lepers who are living outside the village. You must have no further contact with your wife and child.' Ezra wept.

The priest, trying to find something to comfort Ezra, said, 'If you repent of your sins, God may take away the leprosy.'

'But what have I done wrong?' he asked. 'I've always obeyed all the laws, and come to the synagogue regularly.'

'You will have to examine yourself, my son,' said the priest, 'But remember, if the sores disappear and your skin becomes clean and the hairs return to black, then you can come back and be declared clean again.'

'Does that ever happen?' asked Ezra, knowing the answer would be 'almost never.'

He returned to his home with a heavy heart. Rachel came out to greet him, and seeing his face, knew there was something seriously wrong.

She received the news with disbelief at first, then broke into heart-wrenching tears. He longed to comfort her, but kept at a distance – knowing he could infect her. And when Rina came skipping up to them, she tried to embrace Ezra, but Rachel grabbed hold of her and held her tight.

Ezra remembered the parting. Rachel had gathered together a bundle of clothing, and Ezra collected some clay – though he knew he would not be able to sell any more pots. The lepers lived in isolation in a colony outside the village. Ezra had never been there, but knew it was just over the hill beyond the village. He and Rachel made a vow that every Sabbath, when she and Rina were on their way to the synagogue, they would stand at the edge of the village and look towards the hill where he would be standing to wave to them.

As he walked away to join the other lepers from the village, Rachel and Rina stayed rooted to the spot until he was out of sight.

That was twelve years ago. It had been a hard time. The leper colony had been primitive with rough shacks that the lepers had built from wood that the village builders had thrown out. Their clothes were in tatters, and as the scriptures said that lepers were unclean and in a perpetual state of mourning and public disgrace, no one was allowed to give them any new clothes.

There were a few chickens in the colony which kept them supplied with eggs, but they had to beg for most of their food. So they would go into the village, ringing their bells and

shouting 'unclean'. The people of the village would move away in horror – but some would put down plates of food for them.

As the years went by, the leprosy spread over all Ezra's body. His hair started falling out, and what remained became long and lank. His clothes were in tatters, and because there was little water, he couldn't keep himself clean as he did before.

Some of the lepers in the colony spent their time cursing God, but though Ezra felt angry with God, he couldn't bring himself to curse him. He tried to remember some of the Psalms he had recited as a young man. Every Sabbath, he would go to the little hill and watch for Rachel and Rina From the distance, he could see that she was growing into a young woman – and imagined Rachel would soon be thinking about finding a husband for her.

Some of the lepers jeered at Ezra, asking him what was the point of watching for Rachel. He would never be able to be with her again. But Ezra ignored them and kept up his solitary vigil.

One spring, as they walked through the village, ringing their bell, and scattering the inhabitants, they heard whispers about a man who was going round the country, preaching and healing people. Some said he was the promised Messiah. Others said he was a trouble maker.

Then they heard whispers that the preacher had recently cured a leper, and that his name was Jesus. Ezra's heart leapt for a moment. 'How wonderful it would be,' he thought, 'if this Jesus came to our village.' But he realised it was a forlorn hope because there were so many places in Samaria and Galilee, and why would Jesus bother to come to his village.

But though Ezra felt it was unlikely Jesus would come to the village, the other nine lepers in the colony began planning to go and find this Jesus and ask him to cure them. Ezra was happy to go along with the plan – though he wasn't happy about the way some of them cursed God.

They kept asking passers-by if they knew where this Jesus was preaching, and one day, they heard he was expected in a nearby village. Ezra and the other nine lepers decided to set out early in the morning – hoping to get there before the crowds which they had been told followed Jesus wherever he went. It was not to be. As they went along the road, they saw throngs of people making their way in the same direction. The lepers kept their distance – knowing they would not be welcome if they got too close.

When they reached the outskirts of the village, they saw the people were settling down in a large field to await Jesus. Ezra and the others stood away from the crowd and waited – not at all sure how they would get to the preacher.

Then they saw a man in white walking towards them, followed by about a dozen men. As he got near them, they all called out, 'Jesus, Master, take pity on us.'

Jesus looked at them, compassion on his face, and said 'Go and show yourselves to the priests.' He then walked away to address the crowds.

Ezra and the other nine stood looking at each other, not sure what to do next. Then Ezra said, 'I think we should do what he told us to do – go and show ourselves to the priest.'

'But we're not cured,' protested some. But others agreed that this was what they should do – so they all set out to return to the village.

As they walked along, Ezra and the others noticed a tingling in their bodies, and as they looked at their hands and fingers, and down at their feet, they saw that the leprosy was disappearing. They started dancing for joy – scarcely believing what had happened.

They all talked at once – planning what they would do next. 'The first thing we must do is show ourselves to the priest,' said Ezra. Some of them looked doubtful, 'much they've done for us over the years,' they muttered. 'Let's go home first and surprise our families.'

'No,' insisted Ezra. 'The priests first.'

They had travelled quite a distance to see Jesus so it was not until late in the afternoon that they reached the village. Ezra went straight to the priest who had declared him unclean. He examined him closely, and looked amazed to see how clean he had become. 'It's a miracle,' he muttered, 'I've never seen a leper cured before.'

Ezra told him what had happened, and asked the priest whether he thought that Jesus could be the promised Messiah.

The priest shook his head, and said, perplexed, 'Who knows? That is what the people think – but there are others who doubt.' Then he pronounced Ezra clean and Ezra left, joy on his face, and set out to his home. But then he thought, 'Before I go home, I must find Jesus and thank him,' and he turned his steps back along the road he had traversed that morning.

It was getting dark when he neared the village and found the crowds had dispersed, and there was no sign of Jesus. So he walked into the village and enquired whether Jesus, by chance, was staying there for the night. He knocked on several doors, before someone said they knew where Jesus was staying, and directed Ezra to the house.

When he knocked, Jesus came to the door. Ezra fell to his knees and, with tears in his eyes, said, 'I've come back to thank you. The leprosy's gone. My life can begin again,' and he burst into tears.

Jesus laid his hands gently on Ezra's head and blessed him. 'Go in peace my son. Your faith has made you whole.' Then he added, 'But were there not nine other lepers with you Are you, a Samaritan, the only one to return to give thanks?'

Jesus didn't wait for an answer but went sadly back into the house.

Ezra returned joyfully to his village to find Rachel and his daughter Rani.

Luke 17: 11-16

5. The Cynic Confounded

Tom and Andy had been friends for years, but it would have been difficult to find two people who were less alike. Andy was tall and thin, with a mass of fair curly hair and finely chiselled features, while Tom was short and tubby, with straight dark hair and a softly rounded face.

It was not only in appearance that they differed. Andy was an optimist with a sunny temperament. He always expected the best of people and urged Tom to look for the silver lining. Tom, on the other hand, was a cynic. He always expected the worst, and thought there were few people in this world, other than his family and Andy, who had any good in them. And if ever he happened to find someone doing something good, he would always attribute it to self-interest or 'storing up Brownie points'.

It really was rather surprising that Tom and Andy were friends – but they shared a friendship that went back to childhood and a passion for fishing. They also shared a contempt for their neighbour, George, who was so mean he kept his wife and family short of food, refused a home to his old mother when his father died, even though she was unable to look after herself, and would always shout angrily and kick out at any beggar who knocked on his door. For though Tom was a cynic, he had a generous nature, and would help anyone in trouble – while at the same time grumbling about their inadequacies.

Tom and Andy's passion for fishing was a strong and enduring bond, and, whenever they could find a spare moment they would trundle off with their fishing rods and spend a day with their lines dangling in the water – in gentle competition to see who could pull out the most fish. They fished for fun – but the fun was tinged with practicality as they always took home what they caught to eat for supper.

One beautiful sunny day, they set out before the sun rose and went off to a remote fishing spot they both loved. But after three hours they had caught nothing and decided to return home. On the way they encountered a huge crowd walking slowly towards the area they had just left.

Andy, being the more outgoing of the two, accosted one of the men in the crowd and asked where they were going. The man looked surprised at the question. ' Why, we're off to hear the Preacher,' he said.

'What Preacher?' asked Andy.

'The one everyone's talking about. The one who does the miracles. Surely you've heard about him?'

Andy and Tom looked at each other. They'd heard their wives babbling the night before about some man who'd arrived in the area, and was going to hold a meeting or some sort of gathering – but they'd been so busy getting their fishing things ready, they hadn't paid much attention.

They were on the point of turning away from the crowd when the man called after them, 'Hey mate! If you haven't heard the Preacher talk you really ought to come along and hear him. He's really quite amazing. You might even see him do a miracle!'

'Miracle!' said Tom, the sceptic. 'There's no such thing as miracles.'

'Well,' said the man, ' the Preacher's done a lot of miracles.'

'What sort of miracles?' asked Andy.

'Well, he's cured a lot of people, and he's even made the blind see.'

'Have you seen him do any?' asked Tom, always quick to debunk any statement that couldn't be proved.

'Well, no,' replied the man reluctantly, but added defensively, 'But I've got friends that have!'

'Typical,' said Tom, turning away. 'Someone's got a pain and needs a little extra attention – and some man comes along who's a bit different and talks to them. And, hey presto, we have a miracle!' And he turned away, confirmed in his low opinion of men.

But Andy was intrigued, and always ready for a new experience, and said, 'Why don't we go along and hear this man for ourselves? We've caught no fish and we're not expected home till evening.'

Now, people always thought of Tom as being the leader in this rather curious friendship, but it was Andy who had the ideas and made all the arrangements for their various adventures, and Tom, muttering and grumbling to himself all the time about Andy's foolish ideas, would follow along.

So it was that Tom and Andy found themselves walking with the crowd which moved along slowly and amiably until it reached a large circular area which was raised a little on one side. It was then that Andy and Tom saw the Preacher for the first time. He was dressed very simply, and stood on a little rise above the crowds, talking quietly to a group of men who stood round him.

Andy and Tom now had an opportunity to see the crowd as a whole and were amazed to see how many people were there. They estimated there were several thousand people there, all seated in orderly fashion and chattering quietly. They recognised a number of people from their own village, and were surprised to see George, the meanest man in their village, sitting nearby.

The Preacher raised his arms. The crowd immediately fell silent and looked expectantly towards him.

For the next two hours he held them spellbound – talking of the Kingdom of God, and of a God who was like a father and who loved them. He said they must love their neighbour and help even those who had harmed them. They must comfort the sick and help the poor and needy.

He told them many stories – stories far more interesting and lively than any they were used to hearing. And all the stories had a moral to them.

Tom approved – though whispered to Andy that he didn't know anyone who could live up to that sort of standard.

It was difficult to see quite what was happening in the front, but several people seemed to be pushing themselves forward and the Preacher talked to them and placed his hands on their heads – and the crowd craned their necks to see what was going on, and sighs of approval rose from the people.

It was getting late and Tom and Andy were beginning to feel hungry. But they had eaten all their food before leaving their fishing place – thinking they would be home in time for dinner. They could hear people round them muttering that they were hungry and saying they ought to be getting home before they died of hunger.

Then they saw some of the preacher's friends wandering round asking people if they had any food with them – and it seemed that everyone they asked shook their heads and held out empty hands.

Then the crowd fell silent again and they watched as a little boy took a small basket up to the preacher and handed it to him. The Preacher held up the basket, took out what looked like two little fish and several small loaves and held them up and asked God's blessing on the meal. He then proceeded to break them in little pieces and hand them to his friends to distribute to the crowd.

Within a short time, Andy and Tom and all those round them were given food to eat – and they fell on it hungrily and soon felt replete.

When they had finished eating, they saw the friends of the preacher putting all the food that was left over in baskets, and placing them in front of the preacher. Andy was certain he could see twelve baskets lined up – all bulging with leftovers.

The crowd began to disperse – all talking about what they had heard and seen that afternoon.

Andy was full of excitement at the miracles they had seen – especially the way the Preacher had managed to feed the whole crowd out of the two fishes and the five loaves. But Tom, though he had been impressed, declared that it wasn't a miracle.

'Lots of people had food there,' he said. 'It was just that people are greedy and don't like sharing. But when they saw the little boy giving away all his food, they began to feel ashamed, and brought out the food they'd been hiding.'

Andy was a little doubtful about this but could see the logic in what Tom said. 'But even if you're right,' he said reluctantly. 'It's still a miracle if people stop being selfish and share their food.'

'Not a miracle, just good preaching. That man knows how to touch people's emotions,' said Tom stubbornly. 'I bet most of the people in that crowd will be back to their bad old ways again tomorrow.'

Andy said nothing – but remained thoughtful.

As they neared their village they saw George just in front of them. 'I don't imagine that anything the Preacher said will change George,' said Tom gloomily. 'He's such a mean old skinflint.'

Andy could only agree. They'd known George too long to have any hopes of change.

When they got home, Andy and Tom and their wives spent the evening together discussing what they'd seen – Andy insisting they'd seen a miracle, and Tom equally certain they'd only seen a temporary change of heart.

It was the next evening that the tramp came to the village. He was a familiar figure who visited the village regularly. He always went to the same houses – knowing who would help him and who would turn him away. At Andy's house, he always got a bundle of food, and at Tom's house he got money. But he always hurried past George's house because George would scream abuse at him and kick him hard if he got too near. And he would never give him anything – even though there was often leftover food waiting on the table to be thrown away.

This time, the tramp looked particularly unsavoury. His clothes were filthy and he had sores on his face. When he knocked at Andy's door, Andy had to step back quickly as he smelt so badly, but he gave him the usual bundle of food, and the tramp moved on to Tom's house where Tom gave him the usual number of coins. Then Andy and Tom stood watching as he trundled on down the village.

They saw the tramp quicken his pace as he reached George's house and started to walk hurriedly past. But the door suddenly opened and there, to their amazement, was George on the doorstep, with hands outstretched in welcome, inviting the tramp into the house.

Andy and Tom watched open mouthed as the tramp, at first reluctant, accepted the invitation, put his hands into George's and disappeared into the house.

Tom, shaking his head in amazement, exclaimed , 'It's a miracle! It's the last thing I'd ever have imagined George doing.'

'Yes, a real miracle,' said Andy, smiling quietly to himself.

John 6: vv1-15

6. Sara and Ebed – an Easter story

It had been the worst week of Sara's life. Her normally cheerful parents had been plunged into deep gloom. Nothing Sara did or said could lift them out of it.

It was such a short time ago when they had all been in holiday mood, shouting and cheering in the streets. She'd felt so proud and excited that her very own Ebed was the most important thing in the procession – apart of course from her friend. But then, it was as though that day had never happened.

She thought back to when it had all started – to the time when she'd been so ill and been in bed for many weeks. She couldn't remember much about it except that her head had hurt so very badly that she had screamed again and again in pain, and all her fingers had felt like huge tree trunks at the end of her body. Then everything had been a blur until she woke to find a strange man standing by her bedside – looking down at her with such a kind and loving smile that she knew immediately that he was her friend for ever.

Her parents were there too – so happy, the tears were running down their faces. They had kissed and hugged her so hard that she had had to cry out and tell them to stop or they would squeeze the breath right out of her.

And it was on that very same day that Ebed had been born. Sara loved him the moment she saw him. He had lovely soft eyes and a velvety soft coat – and he seemed to take to her straight away, rushing up to nuzzle her whenever she came over to the stables.

Sarah's father said he was to be called Ebed – a servant. She was a little puzzled by the name, but as Ebed seemed to like it and came quickly to her whenever she called, she thought no more about it.

Sara looked forward to the time when Ebed was big enough to ride – and was very disappointed when her father said that Ebed was not to be ridden. He was to be given away as a thank offering for her recovery. Sara couldn't argue with her father – not even when he told her she too must give a thank offering, and must choose her best toy to give away. It was a hard thing to do, but when she remembered the joy on her parents' faces after her recovery, she went obediently to her room to search out her favourite doll with its beautiful clothes.

Her father was an important man in the community, and knew exactly who was in need, and Sara was comforted by knowing her doll would go to a deserving home.

The next months seemed busier than usual. Her father had made many new friends, and there was a lot of coming and going, and very serious talk. Sara didn't understand any of it – but felt the excitement in the air.

A lot of the talk was about the festival which Sara always enjoyed. This year it had been very special – a day Sara would always remember – for there was a procession and her very own Ebed took part in it, carrying the man who'd stood by her bedside on the day she woke from her illness – her special friend.

He was the one the procession was all about and Sara felt very proud as she saw Ebed and her friend go by. Ebed was walking very carefully as though he knew he was carrying something very precious – and the crowds were waving flags and throwing flowers, and palms, and shouting and cheering. And her friend, though he was the most important person in the procession, actually paused as he passed her, and placed his hand on her head in greeting.

Her parents had been very happy and said that 'his time had come. The nation will be saved from oppression and all will be well'. Sara didn't understand quite what it meant, but she was glad for them and for all the people who seemed so very excited.

But it seemed only a few days later that a black cloud had descended. The weekend had started well. First was the special feast which they celebrated every year. Her mother had spent several days cleaning out one of the upstairs rooms which had not been used for a long time. She washed the curtains, and polished the table, and made the room really clean and sweet smelling.

Then, on the evening of the feast, a lot of men arrived and went quietly upstairs. She had seen some of them before talking with her father. Then her special friend arrived. His face was sad, but her gave her a loving smile, and again placed his hand on her head in blessing – and she felt happy and at peace.

And while they were celebrating the feast upstairs, she and her parents had their own little feast downstairs. It had somehow seemed a rather a sad occasion, but she couldn't quite understand why. And she was very puzzled when one of the men from upstairs came rushing down the stairs, and left the house without even saying good-bye.

When she came down to breakfast the next morning she knew something dreadful had happened. Her mother was weeping, and her father looked as though he had lost everything. They told Sara that bad things were happening in the city and she mustn't leave the house.

What a dreadful day that had been. Even the weather was strange and frightening. Such a violent storm broke out at mid day it was almost like night, and in the middle of the afternoon there was a terrible crack of thunder and it seemed as though the whole earth was moving. It was a day Sara would never forget as long as she lived.

Before she went to bed that night, her parents came and sat by her bed, and told her that her special friend was dead. They said he'd done nothing wrong, but had been executed by wicked people who hated him. They said he'd been the most wonderful person they'd ever known, and she must never forget him.

But, they said, weeping, it was the end of all their hopes and dreams for the future.

Sara didn't want to believe it. Never to see that lovely smile again, never to feel the warmth and peace of his touch. She couldn't cry. She crept up to her bedroom and lay on her bed, looking at the ceiling and feeling a misery she'd never known before.

That had been several days before, and a curious atmosphere had descended on the house. People were frightened to go out and her parents scarcely left the house. Callers crept round to the back door and spoke in whispers before creeping away again. Then Sara heard one of them say that a lady named Mary had seen their special friend in a garden. It didn't make sense to Sara. Her friend was dead. But her parents became very excited, and wanted to believe the story, though they said it was very difficult to understand. But, though they seemed happier, they still didn't leave the house because they were known to be friends of her special friend and it might be dangerous. It was all very puzzling.

Then, one evening, all the men who had celebrated the special feast in their house, came again and went to the upstairs room. This time, her parents went too. They told Sara she was to come with them, but she must be very good and quiet.

Climbing the stairs, they went into the room and Sara seated herself on the floor in the corner and listened quietly to all the talk that was going on.

Suddenly, everyone stopped talking. For there, standing in the middle of the room, was her special friend. He looked round at them all and stretched out his hands, and Sara could see great bleeding holes in his palms and another in his side. Everyone in the room looked amazed, and some looked afraid, as if they were seeing a ghost.

Then her special friend, whose name was Jesus, said 'Peace be with you.' He told them not to be frightened, and said he wasn't a ghost, and that they should touch his hands and feet, and see that he was a real person with flesh and bones. Then he asked for something to eat, and one of the women gave him a small piece of fish.

When he had eaten the fish, he started telling them about the future, and what they must do. Sara didn't understand it all, but knew that he wanted them to tell everyone that he was risen, and that if they believed in him, all would be well. He promised them that they would all be clothed with power from on high. She didn't know what he meant, but it sounded exciting. Then he said again, 'Peace be with you. As the Father has sent me so I send you.'

Then he breathed on them saying 'Receive the Holy Spirit,' and the room was filled with light and love. Suddenly Jesus was no longer there but Sarah felt such a warmth and joy that she wanted to dance, while everyone started singing hymns of praise to their Heavenly Father who had resurrected their beloved friend from the grave.

Matthew 21: vv1- 9
Luke 24: vv. 36-50
John 20: vv.19-20

7. Dusty – a story for Christmas

Bert didn't know what he would have done without Dusty. He'd been his constant companion for the last month – and but for Dusty he thought he might have given up altogether. He'd found Dusty in one of the dustbins he was in the habit of rummaging through for scraps of food or anything that might be usable.

Until he found Dusty, Bert hadn't been able to decide whether the owner of that particular dustbin was a kind lady or just extravagant. Her dustbin was always one of the best to look through, and when one morning he found an old overcoat in good condition sitting on top of the dustbin, he felt sure she'd put it there specially for him, because she knew that he was sleeping rough just around the corner.

But then he'd seen the cardboard box. Curiosity led him to look inside, and he found Dusty sitting there looking more than a little bewildered. As Dusty was white, Bert thought perhaps he belonged to the lady's little boy and had escaped. So, picking up Dusty, he climbed the steps to the house and knocked on the door. When the lady opened the door, Bert held out Dusty – but before he could say anything she screeched, 'Get away, you filthy old man. And take that disgusting creature with you.'

Bert had walked sadly down the steps, his illusions shattered. He looked at Dusty sitting quietly in his hand said, 'Join the club, mate. Looks like you an' me's got to stick together!'

From then on, Dusty lived in Bert's overcoat pocket which was large and warm, and

Bert's first act every morning, when he woke stiff and cold from his bed on the park bench, was to put his hand in his pocket and feel that Dusty was still there.

At this season of the year, Bert spent much of his day in one of the city's churches which was warm, and where he could be sure of getting a bowl of hot soup for his lunch. He always shared his roll with Dusty. The ladies at the church, once they got over their fright at seeing Dusty sitting on the table beside Bert, accepted him as one of their 'regulars'.

On Christmas Eve the church was particularly warm and welcoming. Bert sat quietly in a pew, stroking Dusty gently in his hand, and watching the ladies at work. Great branches of holly and red and white flowers were being woven into wonderful patterns round the pillars, and in huge vases by the chancel steps and the altar. Although he had been living rough for so long, Bert appreciated beautiful things, and felt at peace.

Bert didn't know he was being watched by four-year old Susie who was peering at him round the end of the pew, fascinated by the way

Dusty sat so quietly in his hands. After a while, Bert saw her and said , 'Would you like to hold him?

Susie looked dubious and pulled back a little. 'What's his name?' she asked

'Dusty,' he replied.

'Why?' she asked curiously.

'Cos I found him in a dustbin.

Susie's eyes widened at that. 'Where does he live?' she asked.

'In my pocket,' replied Bert.

Susie nodded, as though she thought that was quite right and proper. 'And where do you live?'

At the question, Bert sighed and looked sad, and didn't answer.

'I know where the baby Jesus lives,' said Susie. 'Come and see!' And holding out her hand she pulled him towards the crib at the foot of the chancel steps.

The crib was lit up and very simple. The floor was covered with straw, and the figures of Mary and Joseph and the animals were beautifully carved. The manger was empty, and Susie told Bert that she was to be the one who was going to put the baby Jesus in the crib on Christmas Day.

Bert smiled and leaned closer to look at the figures when, suddenly, Dusty leapt out of his hand and burrowed in the straw. When Bert tried to pick him up, he scuttled down the legs of the table on which the crib was placed and disappeared. Frantically, Bert and Susie searched for Dusty, and they were even joined by some of the ladies. But Dusty was nowhere to be found.

When the time came to lock the church, Dusty was still missing and Bert left the church with a heavy heart. The night was the coldest Bert had ever known and he realised that, though Dusty was so tiny, he had warmed his heart with his love, and had helped to keep him going.

Next morning Bert went into the church as soon as it was opened, but people crowded in behind him and there was no opportunity for him to look for Dusty. He sat right at the back because he knew people wouldn't want to sit near him in his old clothes. Everyone seemed to be happy that morning. People came in with smiles on their faces, and greeted one another warmly, and he felt more alone than he'd ever done before.

Then the organist struck a loud chord, and everyone stood up as the choir and the Vicar processed up the nave. The Vicar welcomed the congregation, and then called all the children to the front. He placed the little figure of the infant Jesus in Susie's hand and led her to the crib. They both peered in and Susie very gently placed the baby in the manger.

They stepped back, and the children, facing the congregation, sang Away in a Manger. As they were singing, the Vicar noticed, from the corner of his eye, a movement in the crib and realised there was one more figure beside the manger than had been there the night before – and this was not just an inanimate model, but a very curious, very white, and very alive little mouse. He smiled quietly to himself for he had heard the story of Bert's lost friend – and when the carol was finished, took Susie by the hand again and pointed to Dusty, standing with the worshippers at the crib, his paws over the edge of the manger, and looking inquisitively at the baby Jesus.

Susie reached in joyfully and picked up Dusty – and then, looking to see where Bert was sitting, walked proudly up the nave with the little mouse in her hand. She handed him to Bert, and said, in a piping voice that all the congregation could hear, 'The baby Jesus has found your friend for you. Now, you're going to have a happy Christmas,' and she skipped happily back to her mother.

It was a very thoughtful congregation that watched the old tramp walking away at the end of the service, and wondered to themselves where he would be spending his Christmas Day.

But Bert was happy. He sat on the bench in the churchyard, feeding Dusty with a bit of stale cheese. He looked down at the Christmas lights glittering in the village below and he bowed his head and said, 'Thank you Lord for giving me someone to share your Birthday with.'

Luke 10: vv 30-37